Lucy Ann Moll

Consulting Editor: Dr. Paul Tautges

Help! I Get Panic Attacks

ISBN
Paper: 978-1-63342-173-8
epub: 978-1-63342-174-5
Kindle: 978-1-63342-175-2

Published by **Shepherd Press**
P.O. Box 24
Wapwallopen, PA 18660

www.shepherdpress.com

Designed by **documen**

Contents

Introduction: My Personal Struggle with Panic Attacks

My panic attacks started with a job promotion. When I became the new managing editor of a health and food magazine, Suzy,[1] whom I replaced, advanced to the role of executive editor. This was a happy day for both of us, right? Wrong! On promotion day, Suzy gave me unsettling, steely stares all day.

Did I do something wrong? Why is she acting so weird? Does she hate me? Will I lose my dream job already?

Confused, hurt, and fearing Suzy's disapproval, I practically sprinted from the office at 5 p.m. Once behind the wheel of my blue hatchback, I cranked up the tunes and zoomed toward the six-lane freeway that would take me to my "safe place": a cozy Cape Cod house that I shared with my husband, Steve, and our fluffy feline. Like Dorothy in *The Wizard of Oz*, I repeated, "There's no place like home. There's no place like home."

As I drove, I tried to forget Suzy's disapproving stares, but they stuck in my head like superglue. Then, suddenly, seemingly out of nowhere, my heart beat triple-time. Sweat beaded on my forehead. I swallowed a lump in my throat. My knees became wobbly, like Jell-O. A horrific sense of impending doom settled on me. Then my mind went wacko as I came to a tight curve: *Drive into the ditch, Lucy. Drive into the ditch. Drive into the ditch.* In panicky desperation, I spoke back to the crazy thoughts filling my mind: *What's wrong with me? Dear God, am I suicidal? Stay on the highway, Lucy. Just stay on the highway. Your exit is a mile ahead. You can make it. You can make it. What's wrong with me? God, help me!*

Three Truths You Need to Know

Panic attacks are terrifying. But you already know this, since you picked up this mini-book. If you don't experience them yourself, you're surely aware of how they affect someone you know. As I share my story and the extreme fear experiences of a few others, I want to help you understand three truths that have helped me.

First, you are not the only one who struggles with panic attacks.

> *No temptation has overtaken you that is not common to man.*
>
> *(1 Corinthians 10:13)*

This Bible verse teaches that we all struggle, including those of us who are "fearful"—that is, who have a propensity for anxiety. The intensity and frequency of our fears may differ, but everyone at some point has freaked out.

Second, panic attacks often proceed from faulty thinking. But by God's grace you can change fearful thinking patterns into God-transformed, faithful thinking. This will require a willingness to trust and obey God, as well as perseverance. Your faulty thinking didn't develop overnight, so it most likely won't go away overnight. Mine didn't.

Third, God promises to help you overcome the fear that precipitates your panic attacks, assuming they don't have an organic, physical cause (more on this later). When you learn to realign your thoughts with God's thoughts, your panic attacks can become a thing of the past. This is hopeful, isn't it?

God can also use your panic attacks for good. Like me, you might begin encouraging others who have panic attacks by listening to them and by sharing your story. This verse in 2 Corinthians is dear to my heart because it gives meaning to my struggle, and I hope it will help you too:

> Blessed be the God and Father of our Lord Jesus Christ, the Father of mercies and God of all comfort, who comforts us in all our affliction, so that we may be able to comfort those who are in any affliction, with the comfort with which we ourselves are comforted by God.
>
> (2 Corinthians 1:3–4)

Perhaps this is difficult for you to believe, but God knows your fears and is able to deliver you from all of them. As you read this mini-book, you will learn practical ways to turn fear into faith. Will it be easy? No. It will require diligent effort. Will it be worth it? Yes. Your fears are one means God can use to help you learn to trust him and depend on him. Addressed biblically, they can become a doorway to experiencing the peace of God which comes through the Prince of Peace who conquers fear.

> When my anxious thoughts multiply
> within me,
> Your consolations delight my soul.
>
> (Psalm 94:19, NASB)

1 Freak Out!

That day on the freeway, full-blown panic attacked me suddenly, out of nowhere. My heart pounded. I became light-headed. Overpowering thoughts demanded "Drive in the ditch" as I death gripped the steering wheel. Was "drive in the ditch" a bizarre escape plan or suicidal ideation? I'm banking on bizarre, since I didn't want to die.

So what exactly is a panic attack? In this chapter, we'll look at other stories of panic attack sufferers: Kari, who had crippling fear of having her blood pressure taken, and Joe, whose panic symptoms prompted an ER visit. But let's begin with a definition.

What Are Panic Attacks?

A panic attack is an extreme fear experience which is out of proportion to the actual situation. Normally, when we perceive danger, it is natural to be struck with fear. The danger we perceive may, however, be real or imagined; our brain doesn't differentiate between the two. Read that last sentence again—knowing this can help with your healing. It is good that your body responds to danger. This is a God-given response to healthy fear, one which enables you to leap into action to protect yourself or a loved one from actual harm. In her book with Elyse Fitzpatrick, *Will Medicine Stop the Pain?*, psychiatrist and biblical counselor Laura Hendrickson, M.D. explains the process.[2] Automatically, your brain registers the danger and sends impulses to the adrenal glands. These release epinephrine and the fight-or-flight hormone adrenaline (and other chemicals), causing a series of physiological events, including increased blood flow.

This fight-or-flight response, however, becomes your nemesis when your fear is groundless. In other words, sometimes what we fear isn't really there but is imagined, as C. H. Spurgeon warned:

> *Such strange creatures are we that we probably smart more under blows which never fall upon us than we do under those that actually come. The rod of God does not smite us as sharply as the rod of our own imaginations does: our groundless fears are our chief tormentors.*[3]

The day when panic attacked me, I was in no real danger. Instead, I *imagined* it. My sense of lack of safety had nothing to do with driving. Rather, its genesis was my fear of Suzy's disapproval and my worry that I had done something wrong. I was consumed by these anxious thoughts and—*wham*!—panic overwhelmed me.

How Common Is Anxiety?

Panic attacks are common and the most extreme expression of anxiety. Statistics show that each year anxiety disorders affect 40 million Americans, ages 18 and up.[4] In any given year the estimated percentages of US adults with various anxiety disorders are:

- 7 to 9 percent: specific phobia;
- 7 percent: social anxiety disorder;
- 2 to 3 percent: panic disorder;
- 2 percent: agoraphobia;
- 2 percent: generalized anxiety disorder;
- 1 to 2 percent: separation anxiety disorder.[5]

Anxiety can be normal in stressful situations, such as public speaking. However, when it becomes all-consuming, it interferes with our ability to respond to the challenges of everyday life.

Panic Attack Warning Signs

Fear is experienced in both our minds and our bodies, causing intense physical responses. These include:

» Pounding heart or rapid heart rate;

» Sweating;

» Trembling or shaking;

» Feeling of shortness of breath or smothering sensations;

» Chest pain;

» Feeling dizzy, light-headed or faint;

» Feeling of choking;

» Numbness or tingling;

» Chills or hot flashes;

» Nausea;

» Feeling detached;

» Fear of losing control;

» Fear of dying.

According to the fifth edition of the *Diagnostic and Statistical Manual for Mental Disorders* (*DSM*-5), which lists anxiety disorders and is the standard used by psychologists and other health professionals to describe and diagnose mental health problems,[6] four or more of these responses must occur at the same time for it to be considered a panic attack. Having two or three physical responses produces anxiety and may signal an impending attack. While some people have only one panic attack in their lifetimes, others have them frequently enough for them to be diagnosed with "panic disorder."

Panic attacks also can accompany some medical problems, which is why it's wise to consult a health professional when you suspect you've had a panic attack. There are known bodily causes, including hypertension, asthma, hyperthyroidism, Guillain-Barré syndrome, anemia, head injury, and drug side effects. But often panic attacks result from faulty thinking that we can change as we trust God, think biblically, and learn to fear him alone. (More on this in the next three chapters.)

Crazy Cycle

For those who suffer panic attacks, our body's response frightens us, and fear increases . . . even when we are not in real danger *and know it*. We perceive the physical response itself as the danger and we dread it. This is when a "crazy cycle" begins. What I mean by "crazy cycle" is that we fear having a panic attack so intensely that when we have a physical sensation like rapid heartbeat or feeling light-headed, our minds go into overdrive and we fear the worst. As we dwell on these fears, they increase. We may think we are going crazy. Often, we have a sense of doom. We may become anxious almost all day long, and as a result we may sleep poorly, exercise less, and consume excess caffeine and sugar, setting the stage for yet another panic attack.

Sometimes we are able to anticipate an extreme fear experience. For example, someone who fears enclosed spaces (claustrophobia) may expect to feel extremely fearful when riding in an elevator. Likewise, a person who fears flying may have great fear when boarding a plane or during the flight.

For the panic attack sufferer, fearful thinking becomes a habitual part of life. Hendrickson writes,

> *When we repeatedly think about fearful events that might happen, it doesn't take long for us to make a habit of those thoughts. Then, very soon, they'll so permeate our minds that we don't have to intentionally think them—they're just there, in the background, all the time.*[7]

We unintentionally train our thoughts toward hypervigilance and nervousness. When this habit is formed, it doesn't take much to bring on another panic attack. For me, driving alone on any fast road, not only freeways, turned on the panic switch. For Mara who feared germs, seeing a discarded straw on a playground weakened her knees and quickened her heartbeat.

How Are Panic Attacks Treated?

When practitioners diagnose mental health problems, they may then make recommendations for lifestyle improvements, such as limiting caffeine intake, better nutrition and adequate water, sleep and exercise, counseling, and possibly medication.

It is my experience, and that of other biblical counselors, that often people who seek our help are already taking medication for anxiety, most commonly an SSRI (selective serotonin reuptake inhibitor) and sometimes a tranquilizer like Xanax. An SSRI is an antidepressant often used by doctors to treat anxiety problems. We do not know exactly how they work. The tranquilizers I mentioned belong to the benzodiazepine family of drugs that work in the central nervous system. These, however, are being prescribed less and less due to concern over addiction.[8]

Consider Joe's experience.

Joe Calls 911

Joe was stressed out from decreasing insurance sales in a downturned economy, and he was short on sleep. As he drove home one day, he began to feel intense facial pressure. Fear took hold, then panic: a rapid heartbeat, chest pressure, and fear he might lose consciousness.

He pulled his sedan into a parking spot and called 911. He dialed his wife and said, "I think I'm having a heart attack. The ambulance is on its way. I love you. Goodbye." Click.

Shaken, Joe's wife called their church where he served as an elder. The secretary reassured her that their pastor would meet them at the hospital. As they waited for the test results, they prayed.

The doctor reported that the tests had come back normal, so he encouraged rest and a follow-up appointment with Joe's primary care doctor. Gently, Joe's wife asked, "Do you think you had a panic attack?" "No way," he replied.

But the next day it happened again. Month after month, as Joe repeatedly fought fear, he made appointments with specialists, spending a few thousand dollars on medical bills. He checked out fine. So he returned to his primary care physician, who prescribed an SSRI. Taking medication was the last thing Joe wanted to do. But he believed he had no choice, since nothing else had provided significant relief. He said the pills helped a little, but he wondered whether he had made the wisest decision.

While *DSM*-5 describes panic attacks (and other anxiety disorders), it falls short in addressing the deepest needs of the human heart and soul. Therefore, counselors who desire to minister to the hearts of those whom they counsel offer remedies that differ from the medical mainstream. Our goal is to point fellow strugglers to the changeless truth of God's Word, which speaks clearly to the issue of panic and how to handle it.

Consider Kari's story.

Kari and Blood Pressure

A trained nurse, Kari knew that her fear of having her blood pressure checked was irrational. She did not have a history of high blood pressure or heart disease. Yet every time she measured it herself at home, or a nurse at a doctor's office checked it, her anxiety was off the charts. So were her physical responses of rapid heartbeat, a sense that she couldn't catch her breath, and tingling in her hands and fingers. Even *thinking about* checking her blood pressure brought on these responses.

As she shared her history with me, I learned that a few years previously, her healthy, marathon-running husband had died unexpectedly from an undiagnosed heart condition leading to a heart attack. Her church had rallied around her and she felt supported. Occasionally a friend remarked, "You're doing so well. You're so strong." But one night, six months after her husband's death, as the Thanksgiving holiday neared "and the Novocaine wore off," as she put it, she awoke suddenly with difficulty breathing and a fast heartbeat. Fearful, Kari took her blood pressure with the cuff she kept at home. It flashed 170/100.

A trip to the doctor's office the next day resulted in tests which turned out fine. She also received a prescription for high blood pressure medication. Nonetheless, she continued to feel anxious much of the time, had trouble sleeping at night, and occasionally had physical sensations of panic. At a follow-up doctor's visit, the doctor suggested an SSRI.

Kari was well aware that doctors commonly prescribe medication for panic attack sufferers, but she preferred not to go down that road. Instead, she sought biblical counsel. As I listened to her story, we agreed with Scripture that her thoughts were overly focused on herself and, therefore, were sinful. Her heart was convicted as she learned that God repeatedly commands his children not to fear. She also learned that an integral part of the remedy for sinful fear, as we'll see in chapters 3 and 4, includes identifying the unbiblical thinking, attitudes and actions that contributed to her panic attacks. As Kari replaced her fearful thoughts with faith-filled thoughts and learned to trust God more consistently, the anxious thoughts that brought on physical sensations of panic decreased.

Since Kari chose biblical counseling alone while Joe used an SSRI prescribed by his physician, you may wonder what is a biblically and scientifically informed approach to the use of medicine. In his book *Descriptions and Prescriptions*, Michael

Emlet, M.D., says that the use of medication is a wisdom issue, since we have been created with both spiritual and bodily aspects that interact with each other.

> *It's not that you can buy holiness in a pill, but using medication in certain situations may help bodily conditions that allow for a greater spiritual flourishing.*[9]

(For a fuller treatment of the use of medication, see the books by Michael Emlet and Charles Hodges, M.D., listed in the "Where Can I Get More Help?" section at the end of this mini-book.)

More of My Story

When I had panic attacks, deep inside I knew what was happening, though this didn't give me comfort. Rather, I experienced greater dread. In my childhood I had witnessed my mom's panic attacks, which were awful. When one came upon her, sweat poured from her face and she complained of a pounding heart and dizziness. She sat on the nearest chair or stairstep, her hands twisting a tissue, her eyes dark with fright. I felt sad and anxious as I stood next to her, saying, "It'll be alright, Mom. Can I get you anything?"

Later, when I was a teen, my mom refused to grocery shop and go anywhere unless accompanied by my dad or me. Xanax was a word used nearly as often in my home as Tylenol or Advil were used by others. So when panic struck me in my late twenties, I phoned her psychiatrist, who prescribed Xanax for me. "Like mother, like daughter," I reckoned. I remember holding the tiny, pale yellow pill in my hand and sobbing. I was a born-again Christian. "Isn't Jesus enough?" I wondered. Of course he is. But did I need Xanax too?

Whether you use medication or have decided against it, or if you or your loved ones have struggled over your decision, please know you are not alone. God loves you. I often remind myself of this verse when I fear others' opinions:

> *The Lord is my light and my salvation;*
> *whom shall I fear?*
> *The Lord is the stronghold of my life;*
> *of whom shall I be afraid?*
>
> (Psalm 27:1)

The psychiatrist's prescription to alleviate my panic attacks began my love–hate relationship with medication. I loved that the medication helped me feel calmer and reduced the physical sensations of panic. Soon the psychiatrist added an SSRI, saying it would replace Xanax. For me this didn't happen. Decades later I weaned myself off the SSRI while under my doctor's supervision, but I still use a low dose of benzodiazepine as needed.

Others aren't so fortunate getting off psychiatric medication.[10] I share my story to encourage you in two ways. First, even some biblical counselors, like myself, may receive temporary help from the careful use of psychiatric medication. We know it is not the full solution, but it can be an aid (one of God's common graces), while learning to trust and obey God and overcome panic attacks. Second, it is possible to wean yourself off medication. If you are taking medication and desire to increase or decrease your dosage, talk with your prescribing physician. There may be undesirable effects from withdrawal best monitored by a health practitioner.

Now that you've learned a definition of a panic attack, become aware of symptoms and statistics, read stories from fellow sufferers, and learned a little about the pros and cons of medication, the next important question is: How can God help you to overcome panic? In the next chapter, we turn to a biblical description of panic attacks and begin to learn of God's provision for victory.

2 Understanding Panic Attacks Biblically

As we saw in Chapter 1, during panic attacks, heart-pounding, mind-racing terror is experienced both in the mind and in the body, often seeming to come out of nowhere—even prompting some, like Joe, to visit an ER thinking they are having a heart attack. So what exactly is a panic attack from a biblical viewpoint?

Let me begin by admitting that the term "panic attack" is not used in the Bible. However, *terror* is often found in Scripture. As you read this mini-book, it will be helpful to think of a panic attack as an extreme experience of fear. Other biblical counselors use equivalent terms, such as debilitating fear, unmanageable fear, irrational fear, or ungodly fear.

Biblically defined, "terror" is an intensely felt reaction to a perceived danger.[11] When the perceived danger is in one's imagination, it sometimes gives birth to panic attacks, even when we know our fears are unreasonable.

So what does the Bible say? Let's look at a few Scriptures about terror, then a passage showing terror in action, before seeing what the Bible says about fear.

Scriptures about Terror

Knowing that the Bible speaks of terror may bring you comfort. I know it has helped me. I feel less alone as I meditate on the truth that God understands intense fear. It can be a great encouragement to know that people in the Bible experienced terror, just as you and I have, and that God met their needs.

> For I have heard the slander of many,
> *Terror*[12] is on every side;
> While they took counsel together against me,
> They schemed to take away my life.
>
> (Psalm 31:13, NASB)

> You will not be afraid of the *terror* by night,
> Or of the arrow that flies by day.
>
> (Psalm 91:5, NASB)

Do not be afraid of sudden *terror*
or of the ruin of the wicked, when it comes.
(Proverbs 3:25)

Who are you that . . .
live in constant *terror* every day
because of the wrath of the oppressor,
who is bent on destruction?
For where is the wrath of the oppressor?
(Isaiah 51:12–13, NIV)

Terror in Action

In 1 Samuel 17 we see terror in action. As King Saul and his men prepared for battle with the Philistines, one of their greatest enemies, the Philistine champion Goliath challenged the Israelites to fight him. Nine feet tall, armored in bronze, and holding a humongous spear, this frightful giant shouted to the Israelites,

> "Why have you come out to draw up for battle? Am I not a Philistine, and are you not servants of Saul? Choose a man for yourselves and let him come down to me. If he is able to fight with me and kill me, then we will be your servants. But if I prevail against him and kill him, then you

> shall be our servants and serve us." And the Philistine said, "I defy the ranks of Israel this day. Give me a man, that we may fight together." When Saul and all Israel heard these words of the Philistine, *they were dismayed and greatly afraid.*
>
> (1 Samuel 17:8–11)

They were "dismayed and greatly afraid" indeed! Did any Israelite experience panic symptoms? Scripture doesn't say, but it is common for soldiers involved in military conflict to complain of intense fear, including panic.[13]

In contrast, David's response to Goliath was anything but panicky. One would expect this teenager to have experienced some anxiety as he tried on Saul's armor, smoothed his stones, and heard the giant's taunts and his brothers' ridicule. Yet his example provides a model to emulate for people who experience panic.

First, he calmly observed the situation. The giant was threatening in size and had a reputation as a fierce warrior. Second, he remembered that God had prepared him as a shepherd boy who protected the sheep and struck down bears and lions. Third, David knew God would prevail over his God-defying enemy (17:34–37).

Is All Fear Bad?

Fear is not necessarily a bad thing. *Rational fear* is good. It keeps us on our toes while we walk in a parking lot at night or stand near the edge of a cliff. Rational fear also prompts us to study for an exam, eat our green leafy vegetables, and get enough sleep. As we noted in Chapter 1, God graces us with this good fear to help us stay safe and be wise.

Another type of good fear is the *deep concern and constructive care* that believers have for one another:

> . . . *that there may be no division in the body, but that the members may have the same care for one another.*
>
> (1 Corinthians 12:25)

You've probably noticed that when a friend says, "I was so worried about you," he or she is usually expressing loving concern.

Of course, *fear of God* is also good. The fear of God is the polar opposite of the fear of man (i.e., people-pleasing, codependency) that infects many a panic attack sufferer:

The fear of man lays a snare,
but whoever trusts in the LORD is safe.
(Proverbs 29:25)

In his book *Anxiety and Fear: A Biblical Perspective*, Stuart Scott defines the fear of God as

> *an acknowledgment and awe of who God is, which causes either full and glad submission to His loving will or terror of his judgment. . . . The one who loves God and delights in Him will fear God as he should. This kind of fear is holy and wise and will keep us from ungodly fear.*[14]

This fear is God-focused; it is not self-focused.

Another good fear is *courageous fear*. For example, you may experience this when a snarling dog is growling at you or your child. Your body reacts physically: your heart pounds, eyes dilate, muscles tense, and you spring into action, quickly finding safety behind a barrier. You may even feel afraid. Scott counsels,

> *Don't make the mistake of equating courage with lack of feeling afraid. The most courageous Christians are those who*

> *feel afraid but place their trust in God and do what He says to do. The question is, what do we do when we are afraid?*[15]

The psalmist says,

> When I am afraid,
> I put my trust in you [God].
> (Psalm 56:3)

But there is a flip side to good fear. This debilitating fear is the extreme fear experience that is the focus of this mini-book. And it is fundamentally a spiritual problem that has ungodly effects.

Three Effects of Extreme Fear

Extreme fear affects us in many ways. It cripples us, tempts us, and demands control in order to provide a sense of security. Let's think about these three effects.

Extreme Fear Cripples Us

Panic can prevent us from fulfilling our responsibilities (Matthew 25:25–26). For example, Mara's fear of germs kept her from taking her four young children to the park, concerned that they might accidentally step on, or touch, a discarded straw or napkin and contract a serious illness. As a consequence, she failed to train her children to trust the Lord (Proverbs 22:6), and went against her husband's desire for their kids to get physical exercise by playing outside on beautiful days.

Extreme Fear Tempts Us

When we're self-protective, we are tempted to commit other sins such as lying (Genesis 26:7) and being irritable. When Joe experienced anxiety, for instance, rather than seeking God's help in overcoming fearful thinking, he demanded that his family remain quiet while he rested in the family room, which also functioned as the children's playroom. If they made too much noise, he yelled at them.

Extreme Fear Wants Control

No one likes feeling out of control. So, when we fear a panic attack, we will probably want to control some aspect of our world.

Kelly, who greatly feared thunderstorms (the roof of her Texas home had been shredded by baseball-sized hail), nervously watched the Weather Station channel on her TV as a storm approached, even though she now lived in the Midwest. She also called her husband to come home early from work so that she felt safe. When he couldn't get off work, she phoned her mom. Had her mom not answered she would have called her sister or a friend. Her desire to avoid the possibility of a panic attack was understandable. Panic attacks are terrifying. We feel vulnerable. Thus, we want to control not only the fear experience but also the circumstances that lead to fear. As a result, we may experience anger, despair, and isolation, and all the while our fears increase and our desire to control quadruples.[16] We want to protect ourselves.

In my case, I feared my supervisor's disapproval. My self-focused thoughts replayed Suzy's stares and I kept asking myself, "What did I do wrong? Doesn't she like me?" My anxious thoughts caused my muscles to tense, my heart to quicken, and my knees to feel wobbly. In my imagination I believed something was horribly wrong with me, and I just wanted it to be over.

My behavior was self-protective. An earthly passion—one centered on approval—ruled my heart more than God did. What about you? Can you identify your earthly treasure? It's another step toward healing.

Ask yourself these two questions:

- What do I fear losing?
- What makes me happy when I think I've gained it?[17]

Once you've identified what you love most, you'll begin to know how to change your self-centered thoughts to God-focused thoughts, as you learn to trust God. The following hymn verse reminds us that God is ultimately in control. He not only is God over your circumstances, but he also brings you healing as you trust and obey him:

Plagues and deaths around me fly,
Till he bids I cannot die;
Not a single shaft can hit
Till the God of love sees fit.[18]

In the next chapter, we'll look in more detail at how the root of our fears is often connected to our love of earthly "treasure."

3 From Fear to Faith

What do all panic attacks have in common? They share faulty interpretations of circumstances.

Three Examples from the Bible

Let's look at a few biblical examples of people who wrongly interpreted their life situations.

The Israelites Who Faced Goliath and Trembled

As we saw in Chapter 2, the Israelites *felt terror* when they focused on the giant's size, armor, and bravado (1 Samuel 17:24). Their wrong interpretation was that Goliath was more powerful than God and his promises.

The Reluctant Prophet Jonah, Who Sulked and Prayed for Death

God instructed self-centered Jonah to preach repentance to the ungodly city of Nineveh. Instead of doing so, he fled in the opposite direction, to

Tarshish. When he finally half-heartedly obeyed and preached an eight-word sermon (Jonah 3:4), the Ninevites responded with prayer and fasting. But like a child who didn't get his own way—that is, the destruction of the city and its inhabitants—Jonah became *exceedingly upset*. He asked God to "please take my life from me" (4:1–3). Jonah's wrong interpretation was that God should serve his desires rather than show compassion for the Ninevites (4:10–11).

Sarah, the Wife of Abraham, Who Laughed Cynically

Sarah entertained the fear that she might remain barren despite God's promise to Abraham to provide them with a son in their old age. When the Lord visited Abraham and reconfirmed his promise, Sarah laughed *cynically* to herself, even *lying*. The Lord said to Abraham,

> Why did Sarah laugh and say, "Shall I indeed bear a child, now that I am old?" Is anything too hard for the Lord?
>
> (Genesis 18:13–14)

Sarah denied her laughter, saying instead that "she was *afraid*" (18:15). Her wrong interpretation was that God was unable or unwilling to miraculously open the womb of a woman who was beyond childbearing years.

Lack of Trust

In each of these cases, the biblical characters focused on their circumstances rather than on God's power and care. They deemed their circumstances to be dreadful. They were concerned that something they wanted to happen—victory over the giant, obliteration of an ungodly enemy, the birth of an heir—might not come to pass. They focused on the difficulties of the future, temporal matters, and self, and so they were anxious.[19]

Likewise, when we become overly self-concerned and, because we are afraid, stop focusing on loving God and others as we are commanded (Matthew 22:37–39), our fear intensifies. In his helpful book *Trusting God: Even When Life Hurts*, Jerry Bridges writes:

> *The circumstances in which we must trust God often appear irrational and inexplicable. . . . We do not know the extent, the duration, or the frequency of the painful, adverse circumstances in which we must frequently trust God. We are always coping with the unknown.*[20]

So how do we get our focus off our circumstances and on to God?

Identify the Root

First, it helps to know the root of our fear. The root of ungodly fear is belief in a lie. The first lie that was believed and acted upon in the Garden of Eden in Genesis 3 set the sickening scene for all the lies which followed, including the suggestion that an earthly treasure can supply what we want, what we believe we *need*.

Can earthly treasure replace God's heavenly treasure of eternal life? Of course not. We know that. But we still keep gathering glittering trinkets. Sure, you may not hanker for an HGTV home or a Lexus. But you may deeply desire one or more of these: peace, security, comfort, significance, respect, love, or approval. And when you fear losing what you desire, anxiety grows like a weed.

> *What was once a desire has morphed into a demand, and it won't be long before you view that demand as a need.*[21]

Jesus, who knows the thoughts of every person (John 2:24–25), also sees our human struggle with anxiety. In the Sermon on the Mount he discusses anxiety and its connection to our heart's treasure:

> Do not lay up for yourselves treasures on earth, where moth and rust destroy and where thieves break in and steal, but lay up for yourselves treasures in heaven, where neither moth nor rust destroys and where thieves do not break in and steal. For where your treasure is, there your heart will be also.
>
> (Matthew 6:19–21)

Name something you treasure that plays into your panic. Is it peace, security, significance, respect, love, or approval? For me, I valued people's approval above all, and when I didn't get what I mistakenly believed I needed, fearful thoughts got a stranglehold on me.

Acknowledge the Truth

There's nothing inherently wrong with wanting peace, security, comfort, significance, respect, love, or approval. Who doesn't want peace? Who doesn't desire love and respect? The problem arises when we want these things more than God himself—his glory, his will, his "Well done, good and faithful servant" commendation (Matthew 25:23).

The Bible teaches that there is only one way, one truth, one life (John 14:6): Jesus Christ. Those who believe this truth and have faith in Jesus have eternal life and experience God-empowered change. But there can be no real change unless you are in Christ. Every Christian believer is in Christ.

Colossians 1:27 contains a powerful promise:

> *To them God chose to make known how great among the Gentiles are the riches of the glory of this mystery, which is Christ in you, the hope of glory.*

Writing to non-Jewish Christians who lived in Colossae in the first century, the apostle Paul reminds all believers that after Jesus ascended into heaven, he sent the Holy Spirit to live within them, never to leave them (see John 14:16–17; 16:7). And the Holy Spirit continues his work in us, perfecting us (Philippians 1:6), conforming us to the image of Jesus Christ. Our once dead, darkened spirits have been made alive, and Christ lives in us.

Belief in this truth and faith in Jesus begins with the confession that we are sinners and have a problem, one rectified only by the Savior. Scripture says that all have sinned (Romans 3:23), and that includes everyone who has ever lived: the Rev. Billy Graham, Mother Teresa, me, you—everyone except Jesus Christ. To sin means to violate God's law. These verses sum up God's law:

> *You shall love the* LORD *your God with all your heart and with all your soul and with all your mind. This is the great and first commandment. And a second is like it: You shall love your neighbor as yourself.*
>
> (Matthew 22:37–39)

No one but Jesus has kept God's law perfectly. He is the only one who has lived a sinless life. Fully God and fully man, Jesus died in our place on the cross, where he took the punishment we deserved. This is why the Bible teaches,

> *while we were still sinners, Christ died for us.*
>
> (Romans 5:8)

God lavished love on us by making the way for us to be able to come to him. To have eternal life and to partake of his divine nature now—opening a door to freedom from joy-robbing anxiety—

you must believe the truth that you are a sinner and that Christ died for you on the cross and rose again.

If you are not yet a Christian, talk to God. Ask God to forgive your sin, as you embrace Jesus Christ as your Lord and Savior. The Bible promises that

> *everyone who calls on the name of the Lord will be saved.*
>
> *(Romans 10:13)*

The moment you receive Jesus Christ by faith, you become a part of God's family. If you have repented of your unbelief and turned to Jesus as your sin-atoning Savior and Lord, then rejoice! You are now in Christ. The Holy Spirit now works in you to cause you to desire to obey God and trust him every moment of every day, even when you're fearful.

Beware of the Progression of Deception

When you suffer from panic attacks, part of what is going on is that you are believing a lie. A foundational verse that can help us reject the lies we believe speaks to the centrality of the heart:

For as [a man] thinks in his heart, so is he.
(Proverbs 23:7, NKJV)

What we think, believe, and desire in our hearts is what we do. The heart is the immaterial part of us. It consists of our thoughts, emotions, and will. So if we feel sad, we may isolate ourselves from others. If we're angry, we may curse. Likewise, when we believe a lie, we act accordingly. Thus, if we imagine we are in danger, we may run and hide, and have a rapid heartbeat and other physical responses to fear.

You didn't become enslaved to the fear that leads to panic attacks overnight. Rather, your panic began (and it continues) because you've entertained fearful thoughts over and over. Unknowingly, you developed fearful habitual thinking. As you made a habit of thinking about fearful events that might happen, your brain created new neural pathways so that even imagining a frightening scenario can bring on the physical sensations of panic. This happens without thoughtful awareness on our part.

But, like me, you can overcome panic attacks by replacing the lies you've believed with the truth. This replacement process begins with understanding how the lie developed. The cycle looks like this:

- » You *listened* to a lie.
- » You *dwelt* on it.
- » You *believed* the lie.
- » You *acted* on it.

Listening to the Lie

The lie leading to terror is this: I need to be in control to protect myself from panic attacks. This means doing what's necessary to gain more peace, security, approval, or whatever it is I think I need. *Remember, the faulty belief is that something other than God himself gives you what you need.* Whatever the earthly treasure, it will never provide what it promises.

Dwelling on the Lie

The attempt to be in control then produces more fear and controlling thoughts, emotions, and actions, and the downward spiral into anxiety (without the intervention of godly counsel) worsens. And so you dwell on anything but what is commanded by Philippians 4:8:

> *Finally, brothers, whatever is true,*
> *whatever is honorable, whatever is just,*

> whatever is pure, whatever is lovely,
> whatever is commendable, if there is any
> excellence, if there is anything worthy of
> praise, think about these things.

Believing the Lie

Listening to the lie and dwelling on it give way to belief—*even when you know your fear is unreasonable!*

Acting on the Lie

Belief turns into action, and the thoughts and actions you repeat become habit.

> *The power of habitual thinking can be so strong in some people that eventually, the instant a thought is produced in their imagination, they register a visceral feeling of discomfort.*[22]

As mentioned above, when you and I entertain fearful thoughts, our brains create new neural pathways, and these pathways become "deeper" each time we think the same fearful thoughts. Brain researchers use the term "plasticity of the brain" to explain this phenomenon. Habitual thinking is almost always a good thing (so, for example, you don't need to relearn daily how to tie your shoelaces or walk downstairs), reflecting the glorious design of our Creator (Psalm 139:14). But for someone afraid of thunderstorms, for instance, the mere suggestion that rain is forecast may trigger physical sensations of nervousness, even panic.

Our neural pathways help explain why panic attacks seem to come out of nowhere, yet our deepest need is the ministry of grace and truth. Because of these pathways, it is like jumping from the top stair to the bottom in our thinking processes. Rather than thinking through the situation step-by-step, we jump from an initial thought to a full-blown panic attack.[23]

As a result of believing and acting on the lie, our fear continues to increase and panic attacks become more common, even making us prisoners in our own homes. Author and speaker Patsy Clairmont speaks from experience and gives hope:

> *After time, I realized that the anxiety controlling my life was mine. I was aware that my lifestyle supported my anxiety; watching sad movies, listening to the same threatening news, calling everyone I knew to talk up a problem. I also didn't eat well,*

stewed over the past, didn't exercise and slept way too much. I woke up one morning almost non-functional. I didn't want to get out of bed, bathe, dress or take care of my family. On that eye-opening day, I made a decision . . . that I wanted to live.

The decision was huge. My journey wasn't easy, but with the hourly choice to move forward things began to shift. With much prayer and strenuous effort, I gradually replaced negative life patterns. At first, it's a wrestling match, but with time it becomes more of a natural response.[24]

In this chapter, we have seen that panic attacks are caused by faulty interpretation of our circumstances. Sometimes, when we make a wrong interpretation, we dwell on the scary possibilities that may or may not happen. Rather than trusting God, identifying the root of our fear, and acknowledging the truth that God cares for us deeply (1 Peter 5:7), we entertain fearful thoughts over and over until they become habitual. But just as we developed this habitual thinking that leads to panic attacks, so we can make new habit patterns that value heavenly things above all.

When we worship God, having no other

gods before him (Exodus 20:3), the false loves that demand our attention—security, approval, significance, and so on—lose their power to enslave us. As Jesus declared to those who believed in him, the truth "will set you free" (John 8:32). God-centered thoughts are the God-given remedy to panic. His love is more powerful than your fears. Though Jesus doesn't promise anyone a perfect life here on earth, if you are his follower he is transforming you into a person who trusts him . . . even in the terror of panic. That's what we turn to in the next chapter.

4 Fear God Alone

My goal for this mini-book has been to help you find freedom from panic attacks. However, freedom does not equal mere relief, though anyone who suffers panic would, of course, welcome such a result. (Maybe we'd even be happy to settle for it.) But most important is lasting change. This lasting change begins in a person when he or she becomes a believer and thus a new creation in Christ (2 Corinthians 5:17). As new creations in Christ, we have all we need to live godly lives . . . without panic.

Typically, this transformation happens gradually. As Patsy Clairmont said,

> *My journey wasn't easy, but with the hourly choice to move forward things began to shift.*[25]

Like her, you and I can have hope that God will work in us to free us from the panic that has enslaved us.

Even better is this promise:

Never will I leave you;
never will I forsake you.
(*Hebrews 13:5, NIV*)

Truly God is with every Christian.

I'd like to say that I immediately looked for a biblical solution to my panic attacks. But many years passed before I learned to trust God *instead of my feelings*. I focused on my distressing physical sensations and feared that panic attacks would stalk me forever. Self-focus was my downfall, just as it was for Joe and Kari.

The solution is trusting God and growing in the fear of the Lord—that is, a deep, reverential respect and awe for God's sovereignty and goodness as he exercises his will. This godly fear recognizes that God is in control of all things and that he cares and is near (Philippians 4:5). We grow in this by developing a sound mind. This type of sensible, sound, self-controlled *mindset* results in sensible, sound, self-controlled *behavior*.

For God has not given us a spirit of fear,
but of power and of love and of a sound
mind.
(2 Timothy 1:7, NKJV)

In this verse, the apostle Paul reminds the young pastor Timothy that God has given him the ability to discipline his mind. Just as God enabled Timothy to fulfill the ministry to which he had called him, so he provides to every Christian his indwelling Spirit—his power, his love, and his discipline to have a sound mind.

So how do you develop a sound mind? By reading the Word which "works in you" (1 Thessalonians 2:13), talking with God in prayer (Philippians 4:6–7), and spending meaningful time with other believers by being an active member of a Bible-believing local church (Hebrews 10:25).

In addition, there are three spiritual disciplines that you need to cultivate.

Watch Your Thoughts

Followers of Jesus Christ are called to live in the world but not be governed by the way the world thinks. In the book of Romans, the apostle calls us to renew our minds with truth:

> *Do not be conformed to this world, but be transformed by the renewal of your mind.*
> (Romans 12:2a)

Transform your thinking by focusing on God's greatness and lovingkindness, and your identity in Christ. Here are a few ways to do this.

» Remember that God has promised to care for you in any situation, no matter how unsettling (Psalm 26:1–6; 37:5; Proverbs 3:25–26; Matthew 10:28–31; Romans 8:36–39).

» Take notes of God's attributes as you read Scripture. In the biblical account of Joseph (Genesis 37, 39–50), for instance, you might note that God is in control (sovereign), orderly, omniscient (all-knowing), wise, and caring, among other attributes. Meditate on God's greatness throughout each day.

» Learn who you are in Christ. Perhaps the most compact place in Scripture where you can read of your new identity is Ephesians 1:3–14. Read this passage carefully. Mark each reference to "in Christ" and "in him." Think about what it means to be God's precious child for whom Christ died on the cross to give eternal life. Also read and reflect on 2 Corinthians 5:17; Galatians 2:20; and Colossians 1:27; 2:9–10; 3:3–4.

Change Your Thoughts

A tool that I find highly useful is the Fear-to-Faith Template that I devised. It recognizes the reality of the extreme fear experience, as well as God's sovereignty, and aids in changing fearful thoughts to faith-filled thoughts. Faith-filled thoughts fill your mind with the truth that you are who God says you are and that God is who he says he is.

The template follows this basic pattern:

Even though ________, God ________. This means ________. I will ________.

In the first blank space, briefly write out what's going on that is causing you fear. In the second blank, identify an attribute of God that counters your fear regarding what's going on. In the third, write a biblically faithful thought. And in the last, choose a call to action.

Here's an example from Dee, a young married woman who feared she'd have panic attacks if she became pregnant: *Even though I am fearing something may go wrong if I get pregnant, God is in control. This means nothing surprises him, I am his child, and he loves me. I will trust God.*

As Dee continued to focus on these faith-filled

thoughts and trust God, she experienced inner peace. Also, in thinking biblically, her brain was making new neural pathways to replace the fearful ones that had sometimes led to a full-blown panic attack.

Put Off Fear, Put On Faith

Back to my story. Stubborn and hopeful, I drove home from work on the highway the next day and the day after that, each time experiencing intense fear. My mind even entertained thoughts of quitting my job. I was becoming a slave to my fear.

So my husband and I devised a plan. I'd stay off the freeway and instead drive the 40 mph roads to and from work. This plan helped to relieve me of my fears and kept me employed, but it failed to solve the root problem in my heart.

» The problem: an ingrained habit of fear.
» My solution: avoid highways.
» God's solution: put off fear, put on an active faith in God.

We came to realize that the answer to overcoming my sinful fear was to unlearn my fear habit and rely on God to provide everything I need for victory. Singing to praise music while driving became one of my favorite strategies to switch my focus from myself to God. I devised other ways to unlearn my fearful thought habit by consciously taking baby steps of faith.

First, with my husband in the passenger seat, I drove a two-lane highway, then a four-lane highway, focusing on the faithful thoughts that had replaced my fearful thoughts. Eventually, I was able to drive alone on the freeway. Trusting God, and remaining in a mindset of prayer, I experienced "the peace of God, which surpasses all understanding" (Philippians 4:7). I continued to practice driving on highways as well as right thinking (Philippians 4:8).

Second, I recognized that I had a faulty perspective. My mind was focused on distracting loves rather than on God. At the start of my panic attacks, I desired Suzy's approval (or at least, not her disapproval). This was my false god. To help me develop a right view of the one true God, I meditated on numerous Scriptures, including Matthew 6:21:

> *Where your treasure is, there your heart will be also.*

In my meditation, I came to see that we obey what we fear.

Third, I trusted God's plan for my life *and* in this test. I learned to see the test (James 1:2–3) as an opportunity to be conformed to the image of Christ (Romans 8:29). Each time I thought (or was tempted to think) fearful thoughts, I immediately asked God for his help and consciously replaced my fearful thoughts with faith-filled thoughts that focused on his attributes, such as his love, goodness, wisdom, and sovereignty.

Trusting God's plan is at the heart of putting on faith. And as you and I replace the habitual fearful thoughts with God-honoring thoughts that revere our Savior, panic loosens its death grip on us.

Remember, just as your panic attacks didn't begin suddenly, God probably won't deliver you from them suddenly, though he could do so if he desired. He has a purpose for your problem of panic and is lovingly using your trial to develop your endurance and change you into the image of his Son (James 1:2–4). As you journey toward fearlessness, take your time. This is a process, not a race. David prays in Psalm 34:4,

> *I sought the Lord, and he answered me*
> *and delivered me from all my fears.*

Conclusion

As you read the stories of panic attack sufferers and of God's plan for you to put off fear and put on faith while your mind is being renewed by the Word, you may already have sensed hope. You may now believe that it's possible for God to deliver you from *all* your fears. I know I do.

I still recall the pivotal moment that marked a significant and wonderful transformation in my own struggle with panic. I was at a crossroads, literally. My bags packed, the tank full, I stopped my Honda at a red traffic light and felt excited, not fearful. And I prayed, "Lord, you know I do not want another panic attack. You know that I've practiced short drives on highways and determined to fear you only. Now as I begin a five-hour trip, whether I get a panic attack or I feel no fear, I will trust you."

For the first time in nearly twenty-five years, I dared to drive on an interstate highway for hours alone. During the long trip I had no jitters, except for a few minutes zipping around a city in rush hour, cars cutting and honking. But when I felt nervous for those few minutes and I noticed my heartbeat quicken, I didn't freak out. Instead, I prayed. I prayed for the other drivers and for my husband and kids back home. Basically I put into practice Philippians 4:4–9.

This passage tells us to rejoice, pray, give thanks, guard our hearts and minds, think about the things of God, and practice the joyful attitude and living the apostle Paul had shown to believers. And it ends with this promise:

the God of peace will be with you.

Yes, panic attacks are terrifying, embarrassing, disorienting, overwhelming, and defeating. Yet through every trial we face, including panic, God teaches us to trust him. As we trust him, out go fearful thoughts, and in come faith-filled truths, such as:

- » God is good (Psalm 136:1).
- » He provides all we need to live a godly life (2 Peter 1:3).
- » He is mindful of us (Psalm 8:3–4);
- » He is for us (Romans 8:31–32, 35–37).

There is hope: Jesus is our hope. His Word shows us the true way of peace as our minds focus on him:

> You keep him in perfect peace
> whose mind is stayed on you,
> because he trusts in you.
>
> (Isaiah 26:3)

Personal Application Projects

1. *Read the Bible daily, beginning in the Psalms.* As you read, intentionally look out for characteristics of God and jot them down in a notebook. Then ask yourself, "What does this attribute say about God and his care for me?"

2. *Keep a Fear Journal.* In it, record the times when you are fearful or have a panic attack. Jot down the date and time. Describe what is happening that is causing you to feel fearful. Also record what you are thinking and saying to yourself about what is happening.

3. *Memorize and review Scripture verses.* Write out the following verses on Post-it notes or 3x5 cards and place them where you will see them throughout the day: Psalm 34:4; 56:3–4; 2 Timothy 1:7; 1 John 4:18. If you prefer, use your smartphone to type these verses into "Notes" and make reminders to review them. Add other Scriptures you discover in your reading which bring you comfort.

4. *Make a Loving Action list.* List practical deeds to do for others in your life. For example, send a card to a loved one, get an oil change for your spouse's car, or take a friend to lunch. Complete 2 or 3 items on your list each week.

5. *Take care of your basic needs.*

» *Sleep.* Aim for eight or more hours daily. Try to fall asleep and wake up at the same times each day. Steer clear of sleep-robbing activities before your bedtime, such as using screens (smartphones, iPads, Kindles, computers, and similar). Note: It is best to avoid long naps during the day, so that you are tired at night and can have uninterrupted sleep. (If you work third shift, follow these guidelines in reverse.)

» *Water.* Drink water throughout the day, but not right before bed. Nutritionists recommend drinking in ounces half the number of your body weight, so a 150 pound person should drink 75 ounces daily.

» *Nutrition.* Avoid excess sugar, "white" foods like white bread, rice, buns, and flour, and junk food. Instead, go for lean meats, chicken, fish, legumes, vegetables, fruits, nuts, and healthy fats.

» *Exercise.* Daily incorporate walking, stretching, and strength training. If you have a sedentary job, talk with a health practitioner before beginning an exercise program.

» *Outdoors.* Spend time outside daily, weather permitting.

6. *Use the Fear-to-Faith Template* described in Chapter 4 and remind yourself of your new faithful thoughts regularly, especially when you begin to feel jittery.

7. *Seek biblical counsel.* Work through some of the resources included on the "Where Can I Get More Help?" pages that follow. You may also want to consider reaching out to your pastor or a counselor in your church. If your church does not have a biblical counseling ministry, search the websites listed with the other resources.

Where Can I Get More Help?

Books

Bridges, Jerry, *Trusting God: Even When Life Hurts* (Colorado Springs, CO: NavPress, 2008).

De Courcy, Philip, *Help! I'm Anxious* (Wapwallopen, PA: Shepherd Press, 2019).

Emlet, Michael R., *Descriptions and Prescriptions: A Biblical Perspective on Psychiatric Diagnoses and Medications* (Greensboro, NC: New Growth Press, 2017).

Fitzpatrick, Elyse, *Overcoming Fear, Worry, and Anxiety: Becoming a Woman of Faith and Confidence* (Eugene, OR: Harvest House, 2001).

Fitzpatrick, Elyse, and Laura Hendrickson, M.D., *Will Medicine Stop the Pain? Finding God's Healing for Depression, Anxiety, and Other Troubling Emotions* (Chicago: Moody, 2006).

Hodges, Charles D., M.D., *Good Mood, Bad Mood: Help and Hope for Depression and Bipolar Disorder* (Wapwallopen, PA, Shepherd Press, 2012).

James, Joel, *Help! I Can't Handle All These Trials* (Wapwallopen, PA: Shepherd Press, 2016).

Kellemen, Robert W., *Anxiety: Anatomy and Cure* (Phillipsburg, NJ: P&R, 2012).

Scott, Stuart, *Anger, Anxiety and Fear: A Biblical Perspective* (Bemidji, MN: Focus, 2009).

Street, John D., and Street, Janie, *The Biblical Counseling Guide for Women* (Eugene, OR: Harvest House, 2016).

Tautges, Paul, *Anxiety: Knowing God's Peace; 31-Day Devotional* (Phillipsburg, NJ: P&R, 2019).

Welch, Edward T., *Running Scared: Fear, Worry, and the God of Rest* (Greensboro, NC: New Growth Press, 2007).

———, *When I Am Afraid: A Step-by-Step Guide away from Fear and Anxiety* (Greensboro, NC: New Growth Press, 2010).

Online Resources

Baum, Cindy, "When Panic Attacks," Today's Christian Woman, September 2001, www.todayschristianwoman.com/articles/2001/september/panic-attack.html

Kellemen, Dr. Bob, "8 Biblical Counseling Resources on Fear, Panic Attacks, and Worry," RPM Ministries, August 8, 2018, www.rpmministries.org/2018/08/8-biblical-counseling-resources-on-fear-panic-attacks-and-worry/

Moll, Lucy, "The Truth of a Panic Attack," Biblical Counseling Center, December 2, 2014, www.biblicalcounselingcenter.org/truth-panic-attack/

Welch, Ed, "How a Biblical Counselor Thinks about Panic Attacks," CCEF, December 21, 2012, www.ccef.org/resources/blog/how-biblical-counselor-thinks-about-panic-attacks-most-read-2012-10

To locate a biblical counselor in your area, visit www.biblicalcounseling.com

Endnotes

1 All names and identifying information have been changed.

2 Elyse Fitzpatrick and Laura Hendrickson, M.D., *Will Medicine Stop the Pain? Finding God's Healing for Depression, Anxiety, and Other Troubling Emotions* (Chicago: Moody, 2006), 122.

3 C. H. Spurgeon, "Needless Fears," sermon first delivered on June 11, 1874, Biblebb.com, accessed May 30, 2019, http://www.biblebb.com/files/spurgeon/3098.htm.

4 Anxiety and Depression Association of America, "Facts & Statistics," https://adaa.org/about-adaa/press-room/facts-statistics.

5 American Psychiatric Association, "What Are Anxiety Disorders?," accessed October 9, 2018, https://www.psychiatry.org/patients-families/anxiety-disorders/what-are-anxiety-disorders.

6 Daniel R. Berger II, *Mental Illness: The Necessity for Faith and Authority*, Vol. 1 (Taylors, SC: Alethia International Publications, 2016), 10.

7 In Fitzpatrick and Hendrickson, *Will Medicine Stop the Pain?*, 125.

8 Drugs.com, "Benzodiazepines," accessed May 17, 2019, https://www.drugs.com/drug-class/benzodiazepines.html.

9 Michael R. Emlet, *Descriptions and Prescriptions: A Biblical Perspective on Psychiatric Diagnoses and Medications* (Greensboro, NC: New Growth Press, 2017), 86.

10 Daniel R. Berger II, *The Chemical Imbalance Delusion* (Taylors, SC: Alethia International, 2019).

11 Elyse Fitzpatrick, *Overcoming Fear, Worry, and Anxiety: Becoming a Woman of Faith and Confidence* (Eugene, OR: Harvest House, 2001), 14.

12 All emphasis in Scripture quotes has been added.

13 Mark Thompson, "Anxiety Disorders on the Rise in the Ranks," *Time*, November 5, 2013, accessed October 19, 2018, http://swampland.time.com/2013/11/05/anxiety-disorders-on-the-rise-in-the-ranks/.

14 Stuart Scott, *Anger, Anxiety and Fear: A Biblical Perspective* (Bemidji, MN: Focus, 2009), 14–15.

15 Ibid., 15.

16 Fitzpatrick, *Overcoming Fear, Worry, and Anxiety*, 57.

17 *Will Medicine Stop the Pain?*, 128.

18 John Ryland (1753–1825), English Baptist minister.

19 Scott, *Anger, Anxiety and Fear*, 14.

20 Jerry Bridges, *Trusting God: Even When Life Hurts* (Colorado Springs, CO: NavPress, 2008), 16.

21 Paul David Tripp, *New Morning Mercies: A Daily Gospel Devotional* (Wheaton, IL: Crossway, 2014), for September 11.

22 Fitzpatrick and Hendrickson, *Will Medicine Stop the Pain?*, 125.

23 Fitzpatrick, *Overcoming Fear, Worry, and Anxiety*, 19.

24 Patsy Clairmont, "Anxiety Alert," PatsyClairmont.com, accessed October 19, 2018, https://patsyclairmont.com/anxiety-alert/.

25 Ibid.

About Shepherd Press Publications

- » They are gospel driven.
- » They are heart focused.
- » They are life changing.

Our Invitation to You

We passionately believe that what we are publishing can be of benefit to you, your family, your friends, and your work colleagues. So we are inviting you to join our online mailing list so that we may reach out to you with news about our latest and forthcoming publications, and with special offers.

Visit:

www.shepherdpress.com/newsletter

and provide your name and email address.